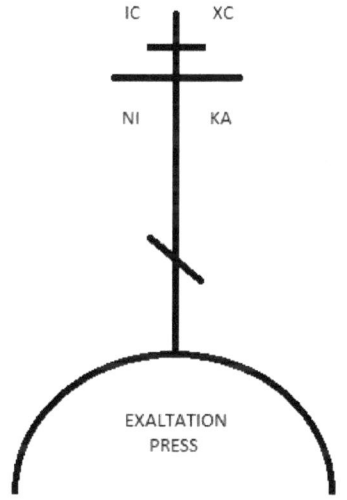

Approved for distribution by the Publishing Committee of the Russian Orthodox Church

From the series "Scripture and Feasts for Children"

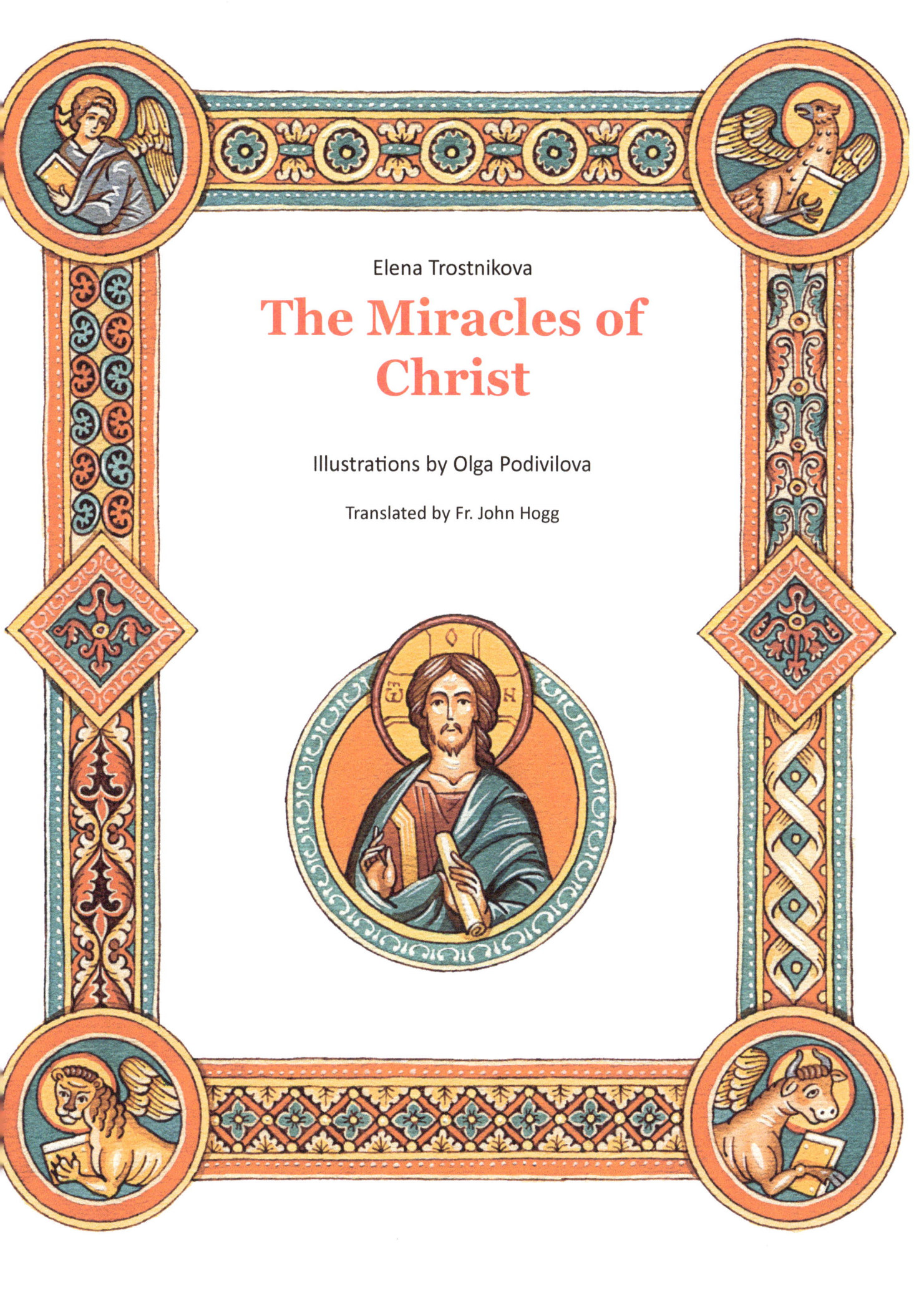

Elena Trostnikova

The Miracles of Christ

Illustrations by Olga Podivilova

Translated by Fr. John Hogg

Copyright © 2019 Exaltation Press

Author: Elena Trostnikova
Illustrator: Olga Podivilova
Translator: Fr. John Hogg

"The Miracles of Christ"

This book is part of the series "Scripture and Feasts for Children." It is about some of the miracles and healings of our Lord Jesus Christ recorded in the four canonical Gospels and is intended for reading to small children. The stories here contained are structured close to the Gospel narrative, written in a simple and clear style for children with the addition of bright illustrations to help children engage as much as possible with the Gospel text.

The book also contains a section for parents on how to read to children about Christ.

All rights reserved. This book or any portion thereof may not be reproduced or used in any manner whatsoever without the express written permission of the publisher except for the use of brief quotations in a book review.

Translated from the original "Чудеса Христовы" by Nikea Press, Copyright © Trading House «NIKEA», www.Nikeabooks.ru

ISBN: 978-1-950067-07-7 (Paperback)

Edited by Cynthia Hogg

First printing edition 2019

Exaltation Press
Grand Rapids, MI

www.ExaltationPress.com

For bulk orders, please contact editor@exaltationpress.com

TABLE OF CONTENTS

Introduction: The Gospel Is a Joyful Book! - 4

The Miracle in Cana of Galilee - 5

The Healing of the Paralytic - 11

The Raising of the Son of the Widow of Nain - 19

The Feeding of the People with Five Loaves and Two Fishes - 25

Jesus Christ Walks on Water - 33

How to Read This Book - 38

Glossary - 49

INTRODUCTION
THE GOSPEL IS A JOYFUL BOOK!

The word "Gospel" in Greek, ευαγγέλιον, means "good news." The Lord said, "Let the little children come to me and do not hinder them, for to such belongs the Kingdom of Heaven (Matt. 14:19)." And no one feels the full force of the joy of the Gospel like children!

The Lord Jesus Christ dwelt among His people, worked miracles for their sake, and wherever He went, the darkness was filled with light. Pain, and even death, melted away. He brought gladness and salvation. He is our Savior.

Everything that we will learn from this Eternal Book is permeated with that joyful child-like understanding that the Lord is with His people, that "God is with us!"

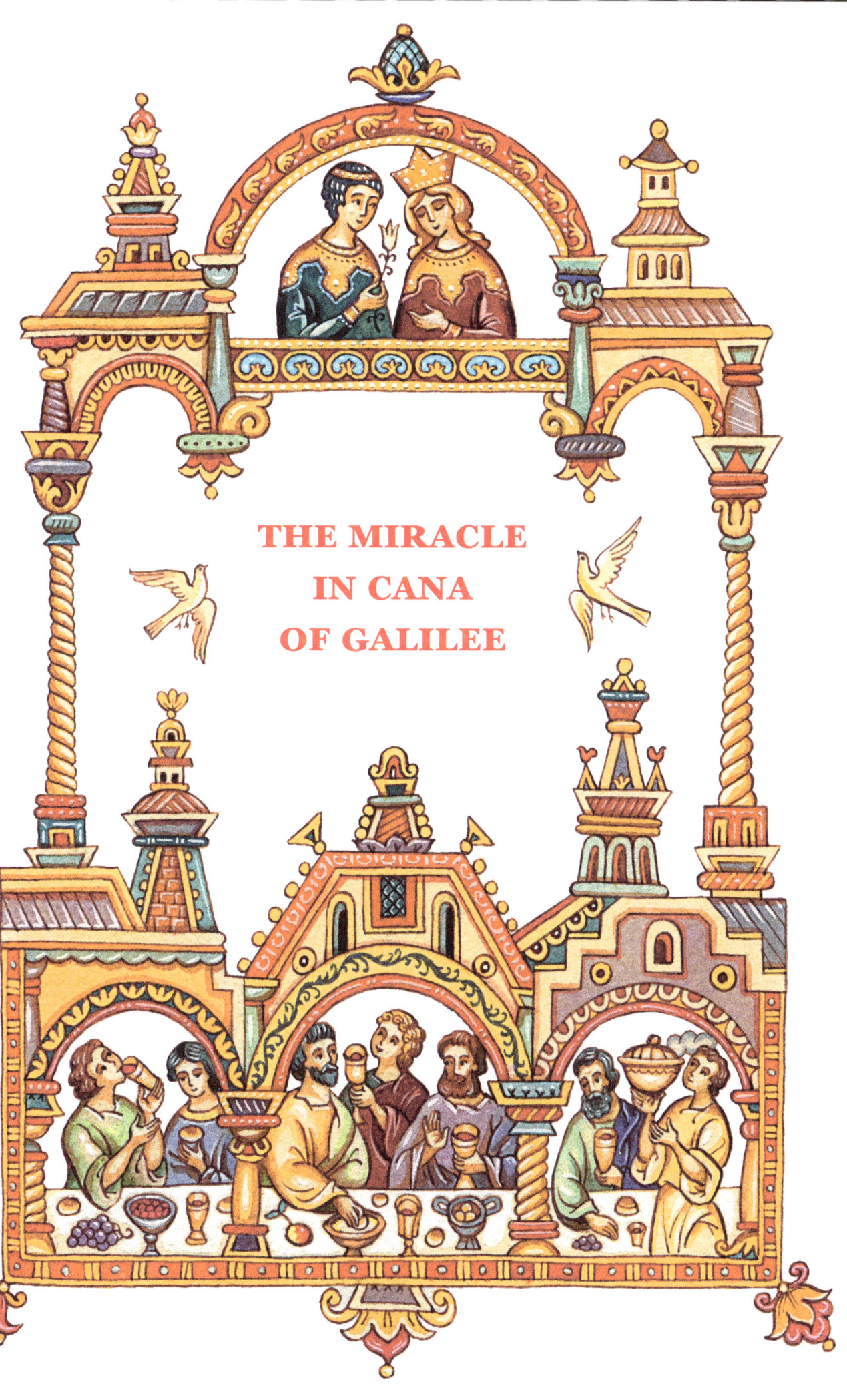

THE MIRACLE IN CANA OF GALILEE

There was a marriage in Cana of Galilee. Cana is a village. In the Holy Land, there is a region called "Galilee." It is a rocky, mountainous region, and those mountains are doftted with villages and walled towns[1]. There is the village of Cana of Galilee and there is also the little town of Nazareth, where the Most-holy Theotokos lived and where she raised her Son, the Lord Jesus Christ.

At the time when our story takes place, the Lord was already going from village to village and town to town in Galilee, talking to people about the Kingdom of God. He told them how to live with goodness and righteousness to be with God.

At the foot of the mountains of Galilee, there is a big lake, so big that people called it a sea, the Sea of Galilee. This lake was full of many wonderful fish and so fisherman lived all around the lake. The Lord's first disciples were fishermen.

But let us go back up to the mountains, to Cana. And so, in Galilee, in the town of Cana, there was a marriage – a wedding.

The mother of Jesus, the Most-holy Theotokos, was there.

The Lord Jesus Christ was also invited to the marriage with

---

[1] Words written in red are explained in the glossary at the end of the book

His disciples.

Suddenly, at the wedding feast, the wine ran out.

The Most-holy Theotokos said to Jesus, "They have no wine."

Jesus said to her, "What is that to Me? My time has not yet come to work miracles."

But the Most-holy Theotokos knew that her Son loved mankind and has pity on us. She also knew that all things were possible for Him.

And so she said to the people who were serving at the tables, "Do whatever He tells you."

In the courtyard where the feast was taking place, off to the side, there were many large water pitchers.

The Lord Jesus Christ said to those who were helping at the feast, "Fill these pitchers with water," and so they filled them up to the brim.

"Now, take some and carry it to the steward of the feast," the Lord said.

The servants took some liquid from a big pitcher with a ladle and brought it to the steward of the feast. He had a sip and then another. He had never tasted such a wonderful drink! After the first few sips, he felt such joy and gladness!

The steward called the bridegroom and said to him, "Usually, people serve the best wine at the beginning of the feast and later, when everyone has eaten and drunk well, then they serve the worse wine. But you saved such wonderful wine for the end of the feast!"

He did not know that this wine was actually miraculous – only a minute before, it had been ordinary water!

All the guests drank the miraculous wine and their souls were filled with joy and light like they had never felt before in their lives. They felt such joy that for years afterwards, each person who had been at the wedding remembered that day as the most wonderful day of their lives.

Thus, the Lord Jesus Christ turned ordinary water into joy for a multitude of people. And that was the first miracle that He worked.

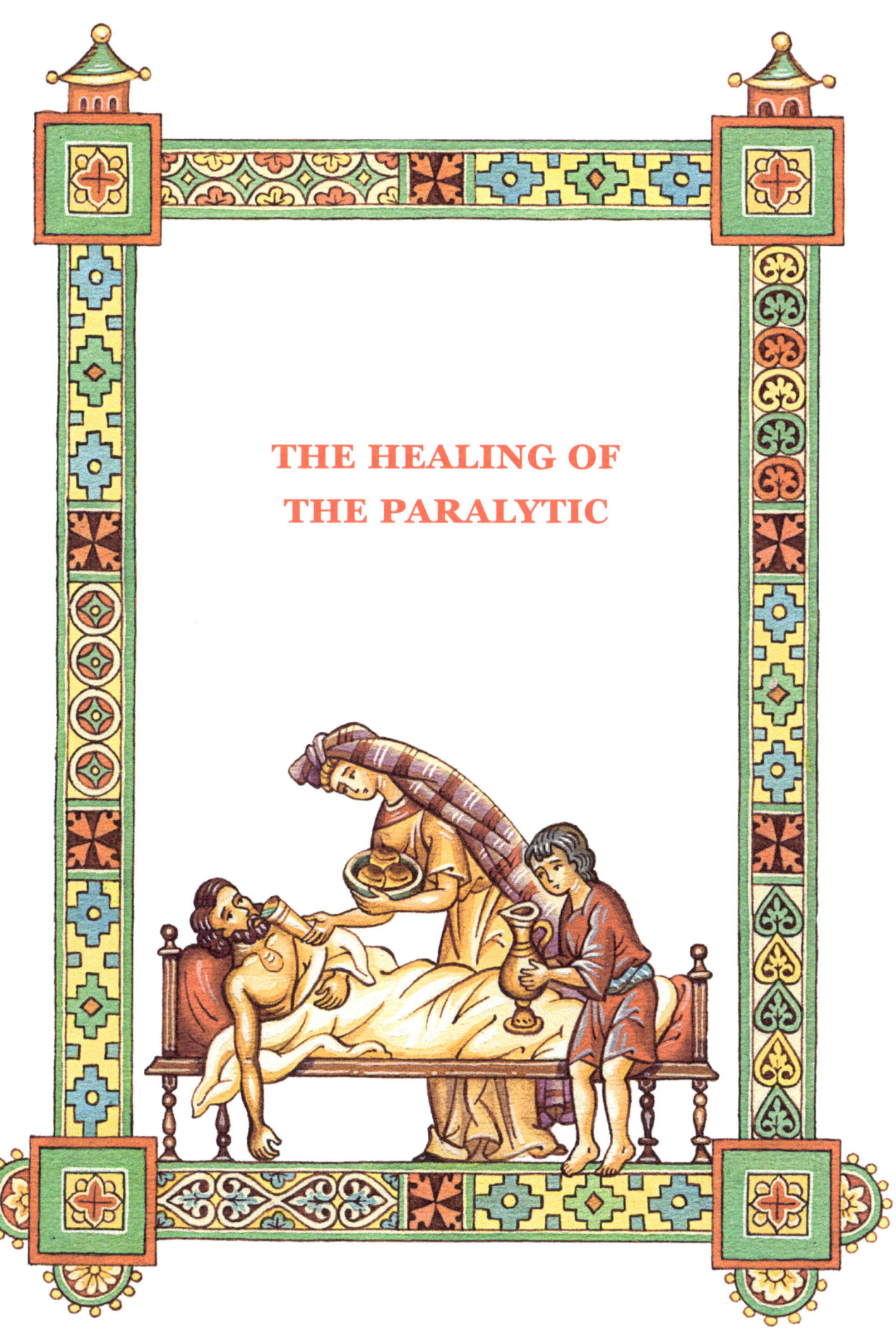

THE HEALING OF THE PARALYTIC

Everywhere that the Lord Jesus Christ went, the sick were brought to Him and He healed them, making them whole and healthy.

They came to Him from all over. Many, many people came to listen to Him talk about the Kingdom of God and to be cured of their diseases.

Once, the Lord came to the city of Capernaum. When people heard what house He was in, a crowd gathered around the house. So many people came that there was not even any more room by the doors. Jesus preached to them.

In southern lands, where it is very hot, sometimes houses were built in a particular way. They built four rooms in the shape of a square with an open courtyard in the middle. The rooms had roofs that people could walk on, climbing up to them with the help of a ladder. But the courtyards were left uncovered. That is where people received guests and went to rest. When it got too sunny and hot, they covered the courtyard with a piece

of fabric or leather, like an umbrella for the courtyard.

The courtyard, of course, had a lot more space than the rooms. But even if it had been enormous, there was no way that everyone who wanted to see and hear Jesus could have fit. They couldn not even squeeze in the gates!

Then four people came to see Him, carrying a paralytic on a pallet.

Paralysis is a disease where a person loses control over his own body. He cannot move his arms or legs and sometimes cannot even speak if his tongue will not move as it should. A paralyzed person has to lay in bed, hearing everything, understanding everything, but unable to move. No one can cure paralysis and those who have this disease live on the charity of the people around them. They cannot feed themselves or drink or wash themselves without help. If someone lays them down in an uncomfortable position, they have to lie there in pain and wait for someone to come and turn them over.

That was what the man was like, whose friends brought him to see Jesus. They heard that the Lord Jesus healed the sick. Even if He cannot cure such a serious illness, they thought, at least our friend will get to hear Him talk, to see Him.

They wanted to carry the paralytic into the house and set him before the feet of Jesus but it turned out that they could not even get close to the door. The door was already surrounded by people who could not get inside. Many people were standing on tiptoe, hoping just to catch a glimpse of the Lord Jesus.

But the friends of the paralytic were not able to catch even

a glimpse of the Lord because they would have had to leave their sick friend behind.

And so, what did they do? They climbed up onto the roof, carrying the pallet!

Even though the roof was low and flat, it was still no easy task to drag a sick man on a pallet up there. But that was not all. The paralytic's friends then folded back the cloth covering the courtyard and looked down. They saw the Lord and heard His words.

Then, when they had opened the roof up wide, they tied cords to the pallet and... lowered it down right into the middle of the courtyard, right in front of the Lord Jesus!

Nobody had ever done something like that before – and at a stranger's house! Everyone in the courtyard raised their eyes and looked in surprise at the paralytic's friends. Some of them began to reproach them for opening the roof without permission and interrupting the Lord when He was trying to speak.

Only the Lord looked down. He looked right into the paralytic's eyes with love and pity. Then He said, "Great is the faith of your friends! Because of their faith, your sins are forgiven you."

People were surprised and a hush fell on the crowd. Many of them did not understand what it was He was talking about.

The Lord then said to the paralytic, "Rise, take up your bed and return to your home."

The man stood up! He took up his pallet, put it on his shoulder, and everyone stepped aside as he walked to the exit.

He walked along the road heading home, with his pallet on his shoulder, and cried, "Glory be to our God!"

It took a minute for the people in the house, who had just

witnessed the miracle, to pull themselves together and realize what had happened. Then they all began to say, "We have seen marvelous works today! We have never seen anything like this before! Glory to God who works such great wonders!"

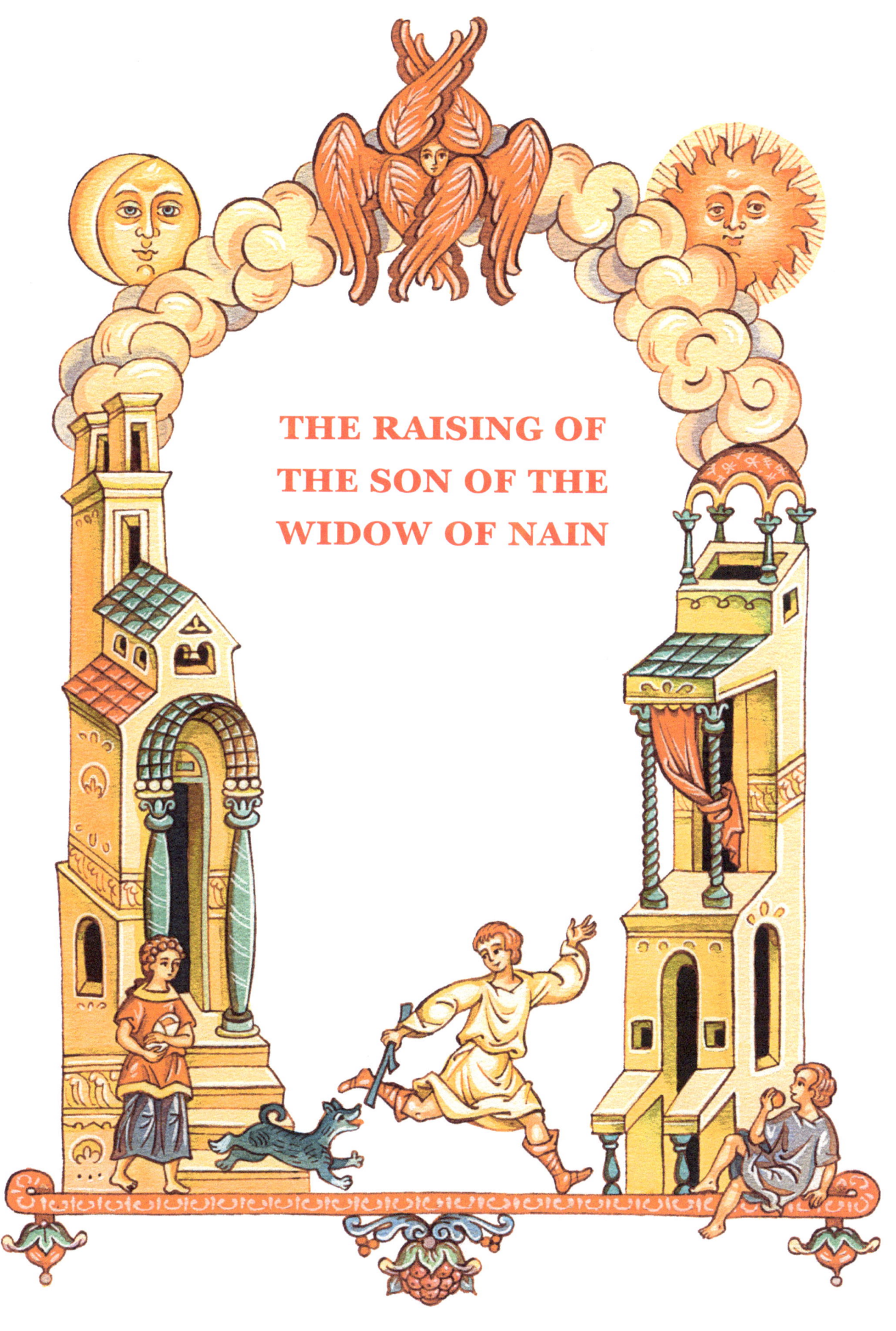

THE RAISING OF THE SON OF THE WIDOW OF NAIN

The Lord Jesus Christ went from city to city, from town to town, and wherever He went, He was followed by large crowds. Many had heard of the miracles He worked and they wanted to see Him and learn from Him.

Once, he went to the city of Nain. Many of His disciples and a great crowd of the people followed Him.

Cities in those days were not as big as they are now. What set a city apart from a simple village was that cities were surrounded by a wall. To enter a city, you had to go through the gates which were locked at night.

And so, when the Lord and His companions drew near to the city gates, they saw that a dead body was being carried out, followed by a large crowd of people who were weeping. Among those following the casket were women crying loudly and yelling.

The woman walking right by the dead body was not yelling or crying. She looked like she herself was dead. It was her son they were carrying out to be buried, her only son. She did not have any other children. And her son was still very young, just a boy. The woman was a widow because her husband had died a long time ago. Besides this son that was dead and going to be buried, she had no one else and never would have anyone else.

Almost the whole city had come out to bury the boy. They all felt pity for the poor woman and mourned with her.

The Lord then saw the woman for the first time. But of

course, He loves each of us more than anyone else in the world and pities us more than anyone else can pity us.

Seeing her, the Lord had compassion on her and said, "Do not weep."

He went up to the stretcher that was carrying the child's dead body and touched it. The people who were carrying it stopped.

He said, "Young man, I say to you, arise!"

The boy, who had just been dead, got up like he had only been sleeping and began to speak! Jesus gave him to his mother.

Fear seized them all and they began to glorify God, saying, "God has visited His people!"

Throughout the whole country they talked about the Lord Jesus, how He raised the dead, saying, "This miracle is from God!"

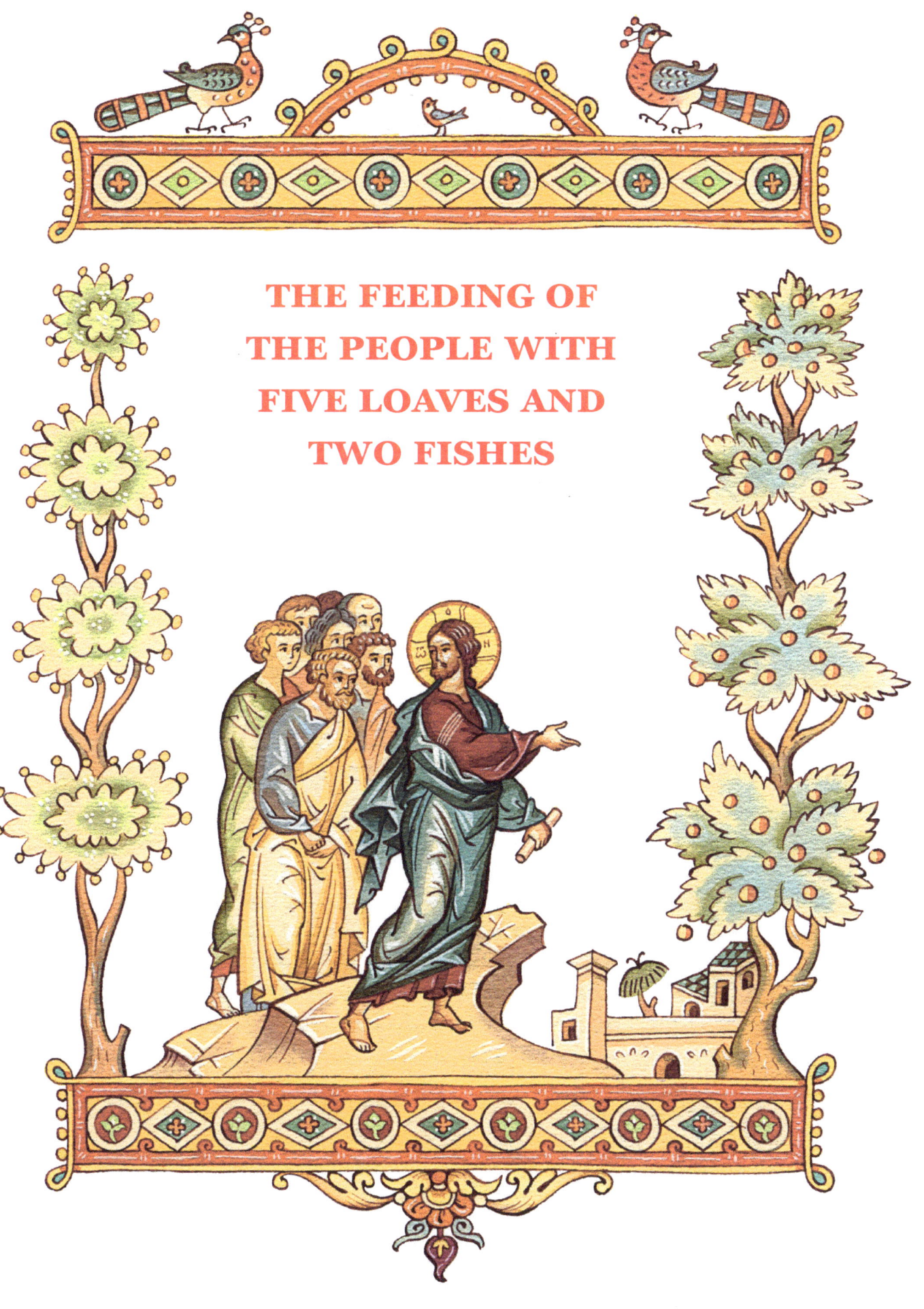

THE FEEDING OF THE PEOPLE WITH FIVE LOAVES AND TWO FISHES

People came from all over to see and hear the Lord Jesus Christ. They followed Him wherever He went. Once, to spend a little time alone and rest a little, He got into a boat and set sail for the other shore, where it was deserted. But the inhabitants of the villages and cities along the banks of the lake guessed where He was going and ran around the lake and even got there first.

As He got out of the boat, Jesus saw the multitude and had pity on them. They were like sheep without a shepherd. They had no one to defend them and no one to guide them.

The Lord healed their sick, taught the people, and spoke to them about the Kingdom of God. He taught them how they should live so they could always be aware of God's presence and do His will.

He taught the people, sitting on a high place, so that they could all hear His voice.

It was almost evening.

The Lord's disciples came to Him and said, "This is a deserted place and it is already getting late. Dismiss the crowd. Let them go to the neighboring towns and villages and buy bread for themselves for they have nothing to eat."

From all sides, more and more people gathered around the hill where the Lord was teaching. He looked at them and said to His closest disciples, the Apostles, "They do not need to go away. You give them something to eat."

"Do you really want us go to and buy food for all of these people?" they asked, surprised. "There are so many of them!"

And there certainly were - about five thousand people! You will rarely see so many people at once. On all sides of the hill where the Lord was sitting, there were people as far as you could see.

Andrew, one of the disciples, said to Him, "There is a boy here with five loaves of barley bread and two fish but what is that for such a multitude?"

"Bring them to me," the Lord said. He commanded the disciples to have the people sit down in groups on the green grass.

When they had done this, He took the five loaves and the two fish. Raising His eyes to Heaven, He blessed and broke the bread and gave it to His disciples so that they could distribute it to the people. He also divided the two fish.

The disciples gave everyone as much as they wanted to eat.

They all ate and were satisfied.

When they had all eaten their fill, He said to His disciples, "Gather up the leftover pieces so that none of it goes to waste."

When they had gathered it, they filled up twelve baskets

with the leftover pieces. That was what was left over from five small barley loaves and two fish!

The people who saw the miracle said, "The Savior that we have been waiting for has come!"

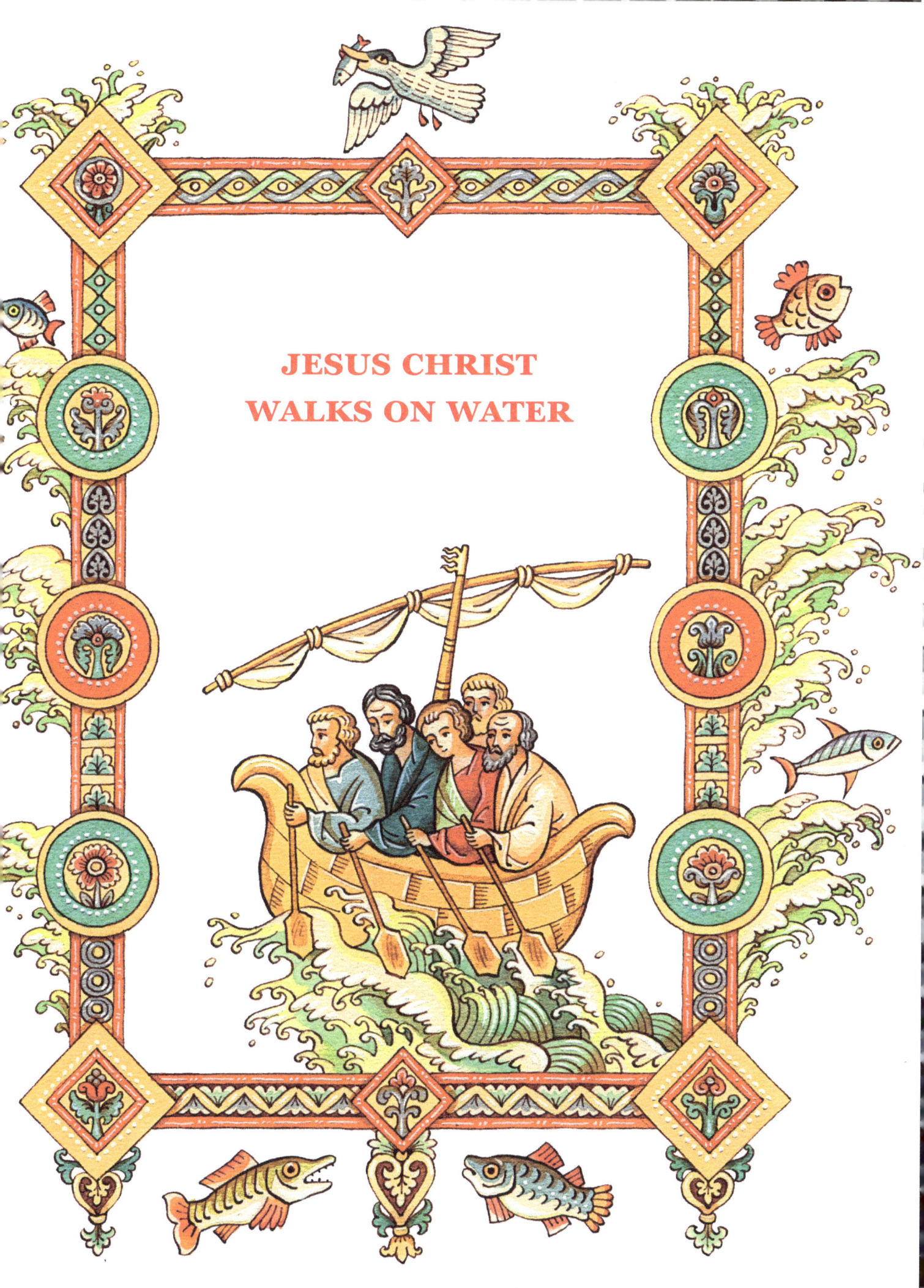

The evening after He miraculously fed the crowd with five loaves and two fish, the Lord Jesus Christ said to His disciples, "Get in the boat and set sail for the other shore of the lake. When I have dismissed the people, I will come to you."

They immediately went down to the shore and set sail in the boat. It was evening. The Lord blessed and dismissed everyone and then went up by Himself onto the mountain to pray alone.

As night fell, there arose a strong wind and the sea became stormy. The waves crashed on the boat and the wind beat against it.

It was dark and nothing could be seen. The wind howled and the waves roared so loudly that the disciples on the boat had to shout to hear each other. The Apostles rowed as hard as they could with the oars but the ship barely moved into the wind. Their strength was giving out and they could hardly keep rowing but if they stopped, the waves would overturn the boat

and they would all perish.

And so, they spent most of the night fighting against the storm but the Lord was not with them.

Suddenly the disciples saw Jesus. He was coming to them, walking right on the surface of the water.

They cried out in fear, "It is a ghost! A phantom!"

"It is I. Do not be afraid," the Lord said to them.

One of the disciples, Peter, called out to Him in response, "Lord, if it is You, command me to come to You on the water."

"Come," Jesus said.

Peter got out of the boat and went along the water toward Jesus. Then he became afraid, "The wind is so strong! The storm is so big! It scares me!"

As soon as he thought that, he began to sink.

"Lord, save me!" he cried out in fear.

Jesus immediately stretched out His hand and Peter grabbed ahold of Him as tightly as he could.

"Oh man of little faith! Why did you doubt?" the Lord said.

They entered the boat and immediately the wind died down. All the disciples in the boat came up to Him, bowed down, and said, "Truly You are the Son of God!"

When they got up, they saw that the boat was already drawing near to the shore where they were headed.

HOW TO READ THIS BOOK

You can read this book even to very small children, including those who are under three years old. That is an age when parents like to read beautiful books with pictures to their children and parents who are Orthodox already try to teach their children the basics about God and faith.

The pictures in this book and the engaging text are designed to tell children the story of five miracles from the Gospels. The first time you read it to your children make sure to set aside enough free time so that you can read it slowly, joyfully, and lovingly, looking it over with your children and telling them the stories. For very little children, you will tell them the stories through the illustrations. You should look over the pictures together in such a way that you get as much sincere joy out of each one as your children do.

The Gospel of Christ is an "unfathomable abyss" of meaning, to use the words of Church hymnography. It is no surprise that even adults can find something new that they have never noticed before in a Gospel book that is intended for children. For that reason, we are including below some very simple commentaries on each of the stories included in this book, as well as some explanations for certain words, concepts, and images.

Of course, our encounter with this book begins with the cover. Who is that on the cover? Show your child, "That is the Lord Jesus Christ" (with words like that). Whether your child has heard of Him before or is learning about Him for the first time, it is good for the child to associate the image of the Lord with His name. Point out how the Lord is standing on the water, right on the waves, and how scared the drowning man looks. Point out how surprised all the fish and birds must be.

When you open up the book, you will see the endpaper, the pictures between the cover and the pages of the book. The pictures on the endpaper depict a big, joyful world, with many characters and objects, and even little stories. If you are able, pause and spend a while looking over these pictures. For things that your child is already familiar with (a bunny, fish, a little boy or girl), ask, "Who is this? What is that?" or "Look! The boy and girl are running and the birds are flying above them! How much fun they are having!" If there are unfamiliar objects, name them for your child. For example, look at the lamp in the top left corner. In terms of the monogram of Christ's name in the lower right corner, you can just say, "These are letters." Later, you can explain that these letters are sacred and special.

Finally, following an image of Christ that is like a little icon, the five stories begin.

Small children may have difficulty taking in the text of the book, or even each chapter as a whole, especially since they are encountering many words that are new to them. Make sure to read to your children without hurrying, in a storytelling voice, almost as if it were a song. First, read one of the stories and spend time looking at the illustrations in detail, starting with what is familiar to them and moving on to what is new and unexpected. Point out and name everything that might be new to them: the bridegroom and bride, the large water pitchers, the ancient city, the pallet carrying the paralytic.

As you dissect each of the stories, discuss with your children what the people are like and how they behave. This is easy to do even with very little children. "Look! Everyone is happy! Do you see how surprised that man is? The dog looks interested, too, doesn't he?"

The glossary in the back of the book will help you explain certain words and phrases to your children.

If your child is eager to know what is in each picture and what will happen on the next page, you can start by flipping through the book once to give them a general overview as a way of drawing them in deeper for a more detailed reading. "We can find out what happened when we read the book." There is no need to try to cram the whole book into your child at once! When you look at the pictures, you can flip through the whole book but if you are reading it, it is best to go one story at a time. You can read more the next time, maybe even later the same day, just not all at once. It is best to stop after every few paragraphs to look at the pictures together and make time for questions. Then read another portion of the text, again pausing to look at the illustrations and answer questions. What is more, both you and your children should ask and answer questions.

Sometimes, children ask questions that baffle us. But is it really so difficult to find an answer? We should tell them what we think and feel rather than looking for the best "pedagogical approach." Even if we say "I don't know," that can serve as an invitation to explore and look for answers together!

If your child is very small and has trouble sitting still, you can go through the book the first few times by retelling the stories in a very short fashion. "Look! Here is the Lord Jesus Christ. And this is a wedding. Do you see the bride and groom? Now they will be husband and wife just like Mom and Dad! Everyone is happy, eating and drinking and talking. A wedding is a big feast. But they ran out of wine! They have nothing to drink. And so the Lord tells them to pour water into these big pitchers. Do you see them pouring the water? Christ prays and a miracle happens! Now instead of water, they have a delicious, sweet drink. They are happy again! The Lord Jesus Christ brought joy to everyone." Of course, this is just an outline for how you could tell the story. The important thing is that you tell it to them while looking at the illustrations, making sure to use simple, sincere language and express genuine interest in what you are telling them.

Most children older than three or four will be able to absorb the text of each chapter very easily and may even be able to listen to the whole book in one sitting.

If your child is an irrepressible dreamer, it is probably best not to read more than one story at a time. Rather, as you read each story, take the time to enjoy all of the details and actions, both the ones depicted in the illustrations and the ones suggested by your child's imagination ("...and then, they all went to the sea and this happened and that happened... And I bet that little boy ran away and got lost and met a talking horse and took it home!"). In such a situation, our task as adults is to redirect the child's attention back to the essence of the story and to the Person of our Lord Jesus Christ. To put it in theological terms, we should make sure that our reading of this book is Christocentric.

If you have children for whom verbal creativity does not come naturally, you may have to lead them into it by asking them questions about the people they see in the illustrations – their personalities, their behavior, what might have happened with them later on...

If your children are a bit older but still not school-aged, you may have to explain different words and concepts more than you would to a younger child and in a different way. We have marked some words in red that you may want to talk to your child about separately and have included explanations at the end of the book. With God's help, if your child has questions about any other concepts in this book, you will be able to answer them independently.

HOW TO TELL YOUR CHILD ABOUT CHRIST

A child's first book about Christ should awaken their interest in and love for the Savior – "Let the children come to me; do not hinder them, for to such belongs the Kingdom of God (Mark 10:14)." We need to support this presence of Christ in our children's lives and rouse in them an interest in His life and His works and satisfy their curiosity. For example, we should retell stories from the Gospel to them. When we retell a Gospel story in our own words, the most important thing is that we use language that is simple, clear, and sincere. Best of all, if you are consistent in telling your children stories from the Gospel, those stories can become a fertile ground for growth in your relationship with them. For that to happen, you should read the Eternal Book to them with love and a special kind of interest that takes into account the needs of your children, choosing the passages that will be most understandable to them and that will touch their soul.

Begin with the events that are the most life-affirming and bright. The Gospel is full of them. Tell these stories very simply, conveying the essence, but in a way that expresses what about the story touches your heart and, of course, is capable of touching your child's heart as well. For very small children, that would include some of the other miracles of Christ (the many times when He healed people, for example) and also the events of His life that are miraculous in and of themselves: His Nativity, Baptism, Transfiguration, and Resurrection.

How wonderful it is to tell children about the raising of the little girl who was the daughter of Jairus, the ruler of the synagogue (Mark 5:22-24, 35-43; Luke 8:40-42, 49-56)! Read the story from each of the two Gospels where it appears. In the Gospel of Mark you will, of course, notice a striking detail: "Immediately the girl got up and began walking (for she was twelve years of age)." In other words, she immediately began to behave like a healthy child. She wanted to move! And in the Gospel of Luke, St. Luke (who was a doctor) notes "He directed that something should be given her to eat." Make sure that figures into your retelling of the story of the miracle of Christ raising her from the dead, along with the grief of the girl's parents and the mockery of those who had seen that she was dead.

While telling the stories, make sure to use the Lord's name reverently and seriously, ideally in the form "the Lord Jesus Christ," so that even though they might not yet be conscious of it, His name might enter their hearts. You should also carefully pronounce the name of the Most-holy Theotokos, the Mother of God. In general, it is good to avoid playing around, using baby talk, or using false mannerisms. Be completely sincere. Then, the stories about Christ will be the deepest part of your common life and you and your children will begin to develop an amazing fellowship in Christ.

The Miracle in Cana
John 2

The miracle in Cana of Galilee is the first miracle of the miracles of the Lord Jesus Christ that we know about: the Lord brought people joy and celebration.

However, some adults have trouble with the fact that the miracle is connected with wine when wine drinking has brought so much misfortune into the world. In families where alcoholism is a difficult fact of life, it is impossible to look at wine with unmingled joy.

But when we read to children, we should do it with a free and peaceful joy. Put aside any doubts that you might have. The point of the story is not that the drink contains alcohol but rather that it is a wonderful drink that "makes glad the heart of man" (Psalm 103:15). When talking to your children, you can compare it to lemonade or juice, or ask them to think of the tastiest thing they have ever drunk. Tell them that this miraculous wine was tastier and more joyful than any other drink because it was a drink from the Kingdom of Heaven.

The Healing of the Paralytic
Mark 2:1-12
Luke 5:17-26

This miracle from the Gospels will help give children an understanding of the sick, suffering, and disabled that they might not yet have seen themselves. Often, we justly try to protect children from the sight of human suffering and illness but we cannot simply fence them off from that. Understanding the love and power of Christ helps us find a way to relate to the pain that is around us. The paralytic had faithful friends who were prepared to do something that seemed strange in the eyes of other people (and naturally will seem strange to children as well!) – they were prepared to take apart the roof so that they could lower their sick friend down closer to Christ. The story of this miracle shows that with God and in God there is no sickness and with Him sin is blotted out. Although it may seem early to talk to a three-year-old about sin, you should not forget about the sins that the paralytic was forgiven. His sins are forgiven thanks to the faith and love of his friends and when the man received his health and fullness of life, the people gave glory to God.

The Raising of the Son of the Widow of Nain
Luke 7:11-16

Here we come to the idea of death. Do your children know about the existence of death yet? If not, then talking about the Resurrection, about how Christ conquered death and has power over life and death, is the best introduction to this unavoidable topic.

The subject of death is a difficult one. There are no uniform methods for presenting it to children. As Christians, however, we possess an important piece of knowledge that is universally applicable, both to those who are calm about death or do not yet understand it and to those who have a heightened fear of it, a fear which even young children sometimes share. We know that Christ conquered death and we know about eternal life. The story of this miracle is a story about Him, the Giver of Life, the Conqueror of death. Use the power of this story and the joyful illustrations to give your child a weapon to use against lack of faith and the fear of death for many years to come.

The Feeding of the People with Five Loaves and Two Fishes
Matthew 14:15-21
Mark 6:34-44
Luke 9:10-17
John 6:4-14

All four evangelists describe this miracle. Here the Lord shows Himself to be the Master of the material world, the Giver of Life. Jesus "saw the multitude and had pity on them and healed their sick." That same pity and love caused Him to give bread to the people so that they could stay with Him without hunger. That is perhaps the most important thing to convey to your child so that you can take in this Gospel miracle together.

Jesus Christ Walks on the Water
Matthew 14:22-36
Mark 6:45-56
John 6:15-27

The story of this miracle follows directly after the story of the feeding of the five thousand. Here Christ shows Himself as the Savior. This is a story about faith and how God grants the faithful victory over even the laws of nature. We know the Savior's words that those who have faith like a mustard seed can move mountains!

The Apostle Mark's words here are surprising: "And they were utterly astounded, for they did not understand about the loaves, but their hearts were hardened." In the Gospel of John the Theologian, Jesus says to the people who came to Him after this miracle on the water, "Truly, truly, I say to you, you are seeking me, not because you saw signs, but because you ate your fill of the loaves." This shows us something. After He had worked such a great miracle as the feeding of the five thousand with a few loaves of bread, it was not only the crowd that looked at it as something mundane and earthly. Even the chosen Apostles saw it the same way, just because it did not fit their understanding of the world. But there was no way to look at the miracle of Christ walking on the water as something earthly! They were confronted with the storm and with their own fear of impending death when they saw the incredible figure of Christ walking on the waters like a ghost. Even more incredibly, they saw Peter endued with the same supernatural ability according to his faith in the Lord and his love for Him!

    Rejoice with your children and be amazed at Peter's zeal! In a little while, you will rejoice in amazement at the appearance of the Risen Lord on the sea of Tiberius, when the same Apostle Peter leaps from the boat into the water and starts to swim to get to the Teacher as quickly as possible (cf. John 21)! Before you do, you may perhaps also tell your children the story of the miraculous catch of fish when Christ first called Peter to follow Him (cf. Luke 5:11). Be sure to read these two stories to your children as well.

GLOSSARY

The monogram of Christ (the Chi-Rho) (on the bottom right corner of the inside cover) - This is an ancient symbol that combines the first letters of His name (in Greek X and P) in the form of a star along with the first and last letters of the Greek alphabet, alpha and omega. In the Book of Revelation, we read, "'I am the Alpha and the Omega,' says the Lord God, 'who is and who was and who is to come, the Almighty' (Rev. 1:8)."

Walled towns - In the ancient world, while there were many villages, there were fewer walled towns. Walled towns, as you might expect, were surrounded by a protective structure that the people could stay inside of during times of danger.

The Kingdom of God - This is a very important concept in the Gospel. In fact, the Gospel itself is the good news of the Kingdom of God. In some sense, even without us trying to explain it to them, children often have an intuitive, child-like understanding about of the Kingdom of God, a wonderful Kingdom where God lives, and their child-like understanding is in many ways closer to the truth than our explanations. But we can add to their understanding that the Kingdom of God is also when we are constantly in His presence and do His will.

The steward of the feast - At great feasts when there were many guests, there was always someone who maintained order and gave commands to all of the servants who waited on the guests.

A water pitcher - In Cana these pitchers were large and made out of stone. To help your children understand, you can explain that the pitchers were "about their height or maybe even bigger!"

Pallet - A pallet was a portable bed that could be carried, much like modern stretchers.

Your sins are forgiven you - The Lord does not immediately heal the paralytic. At first, He tells him something more important: "You are forgiven," in other words, that He loves him. If you talk about this with your children and come to realize together that these were the first words Christ said to the paralytic, coming before his miraculous healing, your own relationship will become closer. For parents, too, first forgive and love their children and then give them gifts and rejoice together.

Sheep without a shepherd - In the Gospel, it says, "When He went ashore He saw a great crowd, and He had compassion on them, because they were like sheep without a shepherd. And He began to teach them many things (Mark 6:34)." Have your children ever seen a flock of sheep? Do they know how sheep gather close to each other and to the shepherd? Even today, a shepherd goes ahead of his flock as its leader.

There were about five thousand people - The words "five thousand people" probably will not mean much to a child. But you can explain that five thousand people would barely fit in a local sports stadium (since they have probably seen a stadium) or you could point out a field or town square about the same size and say, "There were so many people that they could barely fit here! Can you imagine them sitting on the ground, surrounding Jesus Christ on all sides?"

Five loaves of barley bread - Your children have probably never seen barley growing in the field or eaten barley bread. If not, you can tell them how bread is baked out of dough and how dough is made out of grain and what the different kinds of grain are.

He blessed - If your children have spent much time in Church, you can remind them (and point out to them at Church) how the priest blesses things during the Divine Services – the incense, the Gospel, the loaves of bread during Artoklasia, and many other things. And remember, too, that parents can and should bless their own children often with the simple sign of the Cross. The blessings of fathers and mothers, given with prayer, can work miracles.

www.ingramcontent.com/pod-product-compliance
Lightning Source LLC
Chambersburg PA
CBHW051334110526
44591CB00026B/2995